# Dragons

Everyone is painting dragons.

Ramesh paints the teeth of his dragon.

Johnny paints all over his paper.

Ramesh points at Johnny's painting.

"That's not a dragon!" he laughs.

"Don't say that!" shouts Johnny.

"You can't paint a dragon!" laughs Ramesh.

Johnny throws down his brush.
**How do you think Johnny feels?**

Steve comes over. "Stop, Johnny.
It's not OK to hit. Let's talk about it."

13

"He says my painting isn't a dragon!"
says Johnny.

14

"It's not OK to say that, Ramesh,"
explains Steve. "Johnny feels upset."

"You painted your dragon your way," says Steve.
"Johnny painted his dragon his way."

16

"Let's look at all the dragons,"
says Steve.

17

"They're all different!" says Ramesh.
"Yes!" smiles Steve. "Everyone has different ideas!"

18

# Red tomatoes

Katie is at her dad's.
"What shall we do today?" he says.

"Are the tomatoes ripe? Can we pick them?"
asks Katie.

21

"Let's have a look!" says Dad.

"Some are ready!" he smiles.
"You start picking. I'll find a bowl."

Katie feels excited.
She begins to pick some tomatoes.

She picks more and more.

"Whoa! Stop!" says Dad.
"Those green ones aren't ready yet!"

"Oh, I'm stupid!" sighs Katie.

"Don't say that!" says Dad.
"That's not true. You just made a mistake."

28

"But what can we do with the green ones?"
asks Katie.

"No problem!" says Dad.
"We'll put them on the windowsill . . .

and they can ripen in the sun."

If someone says something you don't like, it's important to let them know. "Don't say that!" is one way of telling someone to stop and think about what they are saying.

If you can, explain why you don't like their words. Then you can talk about it together.